DON'T SOFT-PEDAL GOD'S CALL!

Linda McFerran

Books by the same author

CHANGING ASIA
CHRISTIAN ASSURANCE
CINDERELLA WITH AMNESIA
CONSISTENT CHRISTIANITY
ENCOURAGING ONE ANOTHER
GET YOUR CHURCH INVOLVED IN MISSIONS
GIVE UP YOUR SMALL AMBITIONS
TAKE MY LIFE
TAKE OFF YOUR SHOES
THREE MEN FILLED WITH THE SPIRIT

DON'T SOFT-PEDAL
GOD'S CALL !

MICHAEL GRIFFITHS

General Director of the
Overseas Missionary Fellowship

Illustrations and cover by
JOHN RAWDING

OMF BOOKS   ❖   LONDON

© OVERSEAS MISSIONARY FELLOWSHIP

First published	...	...	...	March 1968
Reprinted	...	...	...	March 1969
Reprinted	...	...	...	December 1970
Reprinted	...	...	...	September 1972
Reprinted	...	...	...	June 1975
Reprinted	...	...	...	October 1977

ISBN 0 85363 063 1

Made in Great Britain
Published by Overseas Missionary Fellowship
Belmont, The Vine, Sevenoaks, Kent TN13 3TZ, and printed by
Stanley L. Hunt (Printers) Ltd., Midland Road
Rushden, Northants

ONE WORLD

The nineteenth century
image of the intrepid missionary departing hero-
ically for the dark interior is a dead duck. In today's
rapidly shrinking world, the whole concept of 'foreign
countries' is being changed. The 'foreign mission
field' was never more than a geographical acci-
dent, and like the term 'overseas missions' (what would
that mean to a mainland Asian or European?) now
suggests insularity and the empire complex. In these
days of jet air travel, you can get to almost any country
of the world more rapidly than it once took to travel
from London to John O'Groats by the older methods
of transport. This is a day of great mobility for people
and populations. Whether for education, sport or business, far more people visit 'foreign' countries than ever
before. There are still advanced and less advanced
countries in terms of economic prosperity, but in
matters political and social there is an increasing

5

equality. It is now a commonplace that people the world over, though superficially different, are basically alike in their needs, aspirations and hopes. Among the younger generation at least, there is an increasing sense of mutual interdependence, responsibility and involvement. "No man is an Iland intire of itselfe . . . every man is a part of the maine . . .; any man's death diminishes me, because I am involved in Mankinde; and therefore never send to know for whom the bell tolls. It tolls for thee" (John Donne).

COMMISSION NEVER REVOKED

The 'foreign mission field' then, as once conceived, may no longer exist, but the call to the whole Church of God to go out into *all* the world remains. *Every* Christian is to be baptized in the name of the Trinity, and taught to obey *everything* that Christ commanded—and manifestly this must include the command in the immediate context (Matt. 28.19) to "Go and make disciples of *all* nations, baptizing them . . . and teaching them" in turn to obey everything. . . . This is a general call both to the Church of God as a whole, and to every individual in that Church who is a properly baptized and instructed disciple. That means, simply, that if you are a true Christian, *you* are under orders to go and make disciples of all nations. That still holds in the twentieth century and till Christ comes again.

AM I WILLING?
That all of us,
as the Church of God,
are commanded to go and make
disciples of all nations, does not, of
course, mean that all of us are called to go abroad. Indeed for most Christians it means staying in the country in which we were born. But because of the increased mobility of which we have spoken, there is a greater possibility today that Christians under orders will be sent by the churches in their own country to work alongside the churches of another. Some will go as business men, some as university and school-teachers, some as medical workers, and some as church workers and pioneer evangelists (see 'How shall I go?' page 18).

The challenge, therefore, is obvious: Am I willing to go anywhere that my Master wants me to go? Am I so at His disposal and that of His people that I will do anything for Him? This basic willingness is assumed in this pamphlet because if it is lacking, I scarcely fit at all into the Biblical designation of Christian. But even where willingness is present, there remains the problem of how to know where to go. From being willing to go *anywhere*, to actually going *somewhere* is a major step. How can I know where the Master wants me to go?

But we must first ask other preliminary questions:

AM I NEEDED?

Many of us would want to add the word 'still' to this question. Agreed that there was once a need for pioneer missionaries—but is this still true? Some of us have a further anxiety (perhaps unvoiced because it sounds calculating or unspiritual): "Will the need still exist when I have finished training?" or again: "Will I suddenly find after ten years as a missionary that I am no longer needed—declared redundant, and back at home with a young family and an outdated vocation?"

In various stages of development the Church is now a reality in most countries of the world. The Christians of each country have the primary responsibility for evangelizing it. Do they therefore need foreigners as missionaries any longer? And even if they do now, will they not need less as the years go by? Are not white missionaries becoming 'white elephants'?

"Only missionaries themselves get worked up about the shortage of missionaries and the need for more. Only they see themselves as indispensable!" It sounds a good line, doesn't it? "Some countries today need missionaries as little as—well, our own!" At this point one begins to feel a little uncertain. After all, one of the commonest arguments for *not* going abroad is the tremendous need in one's own country, and the fact that the churches seem to be losing more ground than they are gaining. "If the churches are needy here, that is all the more reason for staying in our own country. We should serve our own people here, just as the Thai do in Thailand, and the Japanese in Japan and. . . ." Can I butt in for a moment, because I have been to the countries you mention? The following observations are far from being a complete thesis, but should help to answer our question.

(i) Even supposing that the Church in Britain were doing very well, would it not still need the help of Christians from other countries? Looking at history, influences from Germany and Switzerland helped the Reformation to get going here. The Moravians were used to help the Wesleys; the Pearsall Smiths were the spark which started Keswick; Torrey, Alexander and D. L. Moody of the United States were all greatly used in evangelism, and recently has there not been a man called Billy Graham? In the missionary sphere the Student Volunteer Movement came to us in the first place from North America. In actual fact, the churches in Britain today are not making much progress and really could do with a few good missionaries from abroad!

(ii) Foreigners still constitute a 'draw'. One of the problems in any materialistic society like Japan, for instance, is getting the non-Christian to listen at all to what Christians have to say to them. Put a Japanese up to preach on a street corner, and nobody pays any attention; but put up a reasonably fluent foreign missionary, and some will stop to listen. The foreigner faces many disadvantages—but his one big advantage is that he is 'foreign' and a 'stranger' and therefore a focus for curiosity, even today.

(*iii*) It is a fact (not a popular one for national pride) that the majority of churches in Japan have been started by foreign missionaries (with national help, of course), and still are. Japanese pastors excel in shepherding existing churches, but it nearly always seems to be the missionary who starts them. This is not simply because missionaries have funds at their disposal and the necessary time and energy, but because pastors of old churches do not find it easy to start new churches. It is rare to find churches started in the first place by nationals. Apathy in his own country handicaps the national pastor. The foreigner does not find it easy but his very 'foreignness' arouses curiosity, and provides an entrance for the Gospel.

(*iv*) Christ *commands us* to go to all nations and this command is not limited to Westerners. Every Bible in every language contains this command. To much 'enlightened' twentieth century thinking, there is something offensively colonialistic and paternalistic about the 'arrogant' Westerner preaching the Gospel to the ignorant 'natives'. But that concept has long since been replaced by that of a completely international and mutually responsible Christian Church. Hitherto the West has gone to the East, the European has gone to Africa, and the American to Asia. Is there not now a place for the African to go to the 'natives' of Great Britain, and the Asian to go to the 'natives' of North and South America? Why on earth not? You expect it in Heaven! An international Church, I mean. It now needs to be made clear that the Church is an international mission to mankind. If your missionary team in Japan, Egypt, France, London or downtown Liverpool consists of an African, an Indian, a Filipino, a Peruvian and a Norwegian, people with different backgrounds, education, race and nationality, yet manifesting in practice the harmony that Christ brings, what a potent force there is here, with a highly contemporary message to a world rent by nationalism and racial issues.

(v) Missionaries are still needed ˉin considerable numbers. Just because a church exists in a country this does not mean that the task of evangelism is nearly finished: it may only just have begun. In 1885 Verbeck calculated that after 1900 no more missionaries would be needed in Japan—the job would be done. Yet with over 2,000 missionaries still at work today in that country, the Church still numbers less than one per cent of the population. Moreover, even if a church grows in one generation, there may be a recession in the next. If a country is 'evangelized' in one generation, it will need evangelizing again in the next. But many, many lands have not yet been fully evangelized in any generation! Thailand is a case in point; the Church there is so small and weak that the country remains largely unevangelized.

In the providence of God, He allows some fields to become entirely closed to the Gospel. In others as the church becomes strong the type of missionary required may change. Even so, there can be few countries where a worker with long experience and fluency in the language is not respected and invited to remain, though workers may need to be re-trained for fresh deployment or assignment. Yes, workers are in very short supply.

AM I ELIGIBLE?

Every dedicated Christian ought to be willing to go anywhere. But not every Christian is fitted for the task. Consider some of the factors involved:

(*i*) *Health.* A man who is a museum of pathological conditions, and yet willing to go, would be a liability where medical facilities are inadequate. A missionary needs to be strong and fit in order to adjust to a new and difficult climate. He needs to be able to face late night duties and yet rise early the following day. He may have to accept an unfamiliar and uncongenial diet, and irregular mealtimes. He will need strong knees for squatting on the floor and a strong back for digging cars out of the mud, or houses out of the snow. On the other hand, he does not need to look like a 'You, too, can have a body like mine' advert. Westerners often appear too large as it is in some overseas contexts, while people of slighter build are less conspicuous and find it easier to identify with the people.

(*ii*) *Family.* A Christian with eighteen children might be willing to go anywhere, but he could scarcely expect any responsible mission to view him as a candidate with

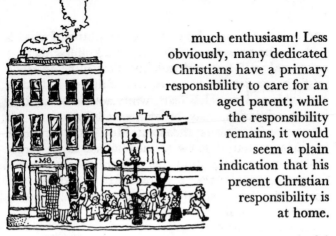

much enthusiasm! Less obviously, many dedicated Christians have a primary responsibility to care for an aged parent; while the responsibility remains, it would seem a plain indication that his present Christian responsibility is at home.

(iii) Stability. William Cowper was a wonderful hymn-writer, but suffered from bouts of severe mental depression, which would have disqualified him from missionary service, but his ex-sailor friend, John Newton, would have fitted the bill well.

All missionaries are subjected to an increased nervous strain. Even under normal conditions there may be initial culture shock while becoming accustomed to unfamiliar foods and customs, and the sense of alienation

and isolation caused by understanding little of what is said. Under pressure people may crack unless there is emotional resilience and stability. Fear of being alone in the house, fear of strangers, fear of illness, and other nameable and nameless fears, while not abnormal in a familiar situation, may become magnified out of all proportion in an overseas context. Most of the first CIM missionaries that I knew seemed to me to be large, six-foot, phlegmatic, front row forward, none-of-these-things-move-me types. I feared that I was far too imaginative and excitable to pass the test. Even a course on tropical diseases made me nervous! However, sensitivity and imagination are also useful qualities in a missionary. The unimaginative person may have few fears but often lacks sensitivity. The answer probably is that not all missionaries are called to be pioneers in rugged places: the Lord fits men as instruments for the kind of work to which He has called them. Clearly, an over-excitable or nervous temperament  would call for investigation, while a family or personal history of nervous illness might indicate unsuitability.

(iv) Intellectual ability. Now, of course, if you are a very gifted intellectual person, it would be an absolute waste . . . for you to stay at home, unless you are sure that that is the Lord's will. No qualifications, however high, would be a waste overseas. The 'brain drain' shows that people who are brilliant in some field are appreciated anywhere, regardless of their national origins. The Church of Christ needs its best brains to spearhead its main advances. If it takes a good brain to teach in one's own tongue, it takes a better one to teach in a foreign language with a different set of thought patterns —especially in a subject like theology.

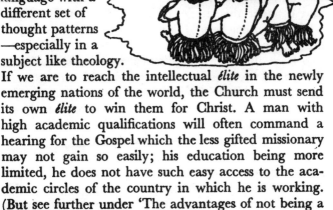

If we are to reach the intellectual *élite* in the newly emerging nations of the world, the Church must send its own *élite* to win them for Christ. A man with high academic qualifications will often command a hearing for the Gospel which the less gifted missionary may not gain so easily; his education being more limited, he does not have such easy access to the academic circles of the country in which he is working. (But see further under 'The advantages of not being a missionary' p. 19.)

But what if you are not an 'egghead'? There is still plenty to be done, and the most effective missionary is not necessarily the one with lots of grey matter and gifted patter. It is warm sincerity, practical Christian

love and genuine interest in others which carry the day and conquer the citadel of another's heart for Jesus. There are other keys to open doors, and doors to open other than academic ones. It may be your experience in a trade union or in a practical trade, your ability to draw good pictures, or make friends with strangers, to play some sport really well, or even the pursuit of a favourite hobby, which the Lord will use to open doors.

(v) *Initiative*. Are you any earthly use? Are you active in your own church? Has God used you so that others have become Christians through you? A missionary does not have to be an egghead, but he ought to be a soul-winner. Most people can go along with an existing church or group. It takes little initiative to climb on the band wagon. But if you were to find yourself in an area with no church, or a factory with no Christian union, would you start one? Have you ever started anything and got it moving—a house-meeting, a Bible study group, or a Christian union?

Missionaries often need to be initiators and improvisators, too. If you are already an initiator as well as an active participator, you are the kind of person the overseas churches need: a breaker down of barriers, a disturber of inertia, a catalyst of fresh surges of activity.

Two extremes are to be avoided: (a) the rare person with an over-confident Messianic complex who feels that once he arrives, the whole situation will be transformed; (b) the far more common opposite extreme of over-diffidence—the person so conscious of human inability that he underestimates the power of God. We should certainly be humble, not just in recognizing our own limitations, but also in listening to others' assessment of our potentialities. If our fellow-Christians invite us to undertake some task, presumably they judge that we have some contribution to make.

(*vi*) *Language learning.* School language learning, whether languishing with Latin or groaning with Greek, gives no indication of what you can do in a living language situation where you are continually hearing new words in an everyday context. Certainly there are many places where English can be used, but in most countries new languages must still be learnt if we are to reach men's hearts and understand their thought patterns.

Well, supposing one passes all these tests satisfactorily and is not disqualified as a physical wreck or a psychological risk, supposing there are no home ties, and some indication of usefulness in the church at home, there are still other matters which need to be sorted out.

HOW SHALL I GO?

Shall I go as a missionary, or in some other capacity but intending to use every opportunity that I can for Christian work (i.e. as a Christian Witness Overseas—

C.W.O. for short)? This question is especially pointed when it is a choice between a Christian and a government hospital, or between a mission school and a state school. If the work done is the same, why should the one reckon as a "missionary" and the other not, merely because the method of support is different? Perhaps we can summarize the matter in this way:

(*a*) Some countries are entirely closed to missionaries and the only way to get a Christian witness in is in some professional capacity, such as a lecturer, engineer or business man. Here there may be no choice.

(*b*) In other situations either mode of entry is possible. So . . .

(*i*) Ask yourself: "What am I called to *do?*" If your primary aim is to plant and nourish churches then, without question, you should go as a missionary so that you may give all your time to this form of service.

(*ii*) Consider the advantages of not being a missionary:

(a) The absence of the financial motive in Christian service. This may mean a great deal in a country where the religious 'professionals' serve for a livelihood, and so Christian ministers may be tarred with the same brush.

(b) Access to professional, academic or business circles normally closed to all but the most outstanding missionaries, and a very wide range of contacts with non-Christians.

(c) The opportunity to maintain a higher standard of living, to enjoy comfort and to rise in one's professional sphere. (Perhaps you detect some irony at this point! for such a pathway *may* be chosen as a way of compromise when there is unwillingness to sacrifice security or living standards for the gospel's sake.)

(*iii*) Consider the disadvantages of not being a missionary:

(a) You are trying to do two jobs at once. For most men of average ability, this means ending up by doing neither very well, or by one crowding out the other. Men of outstanding ability have done both with amazing success, and these are always the examples quoted to prove what *can* be done. Such men can. Can you?

(b) You are too busy doing your main job ever to learn a language well. This will limit your effectiveness in many countries, where English is not the real language of the heart.

(c) Your employers may keep moving you about so that you never get time to settle down in any one place and do a really good job: this can be extremely frustrating. Nevertheless some become C.W.O.s under the impression that they will have 'strategic opportunities' and end up achieving nothing at all.

(d) The social round and the standard of living expected of expatriates may effectively cut you off from the people, and end in complete failure to identify with the people of the country.

(e) What you have been able to do in your own country is no measure of what you can do in more exacting circumstances and in a tropical climate.

Before we choose the C.W.O. path, we need to be quite sure of our motives—that we are not evading the sacrifice of identification with an alien culture, acceptance of a lower standard of living or the humiliation of having to live 'on charity'. It is not too difficult to discover if one's motives are pure or not, provided one is utterly open to follow the Lord's leading.

AM I REALLY CALLED?

Here is the main issue. I am willing to go anywhere, but how can I be sure that it is really God's will for me to go abroad to some specific place or type of work? Perhaps this can best be answered by asking:

Who is going to call you?

Why, the Lord, of course.

Yes, but how?

Well, I suppose He will let me know somehow.

How?

Well, perhaps by a dream or a vision, but more probably by a verse or. . . ?

Is your going to the mission field then to depend solely on your subjective sense of God's calling? Is that verse alone decisive, or is it just confirmatory? What does the New Testament teach?

Let me give you a suggested conclusion and then the evidence upon which it is based.

Not one of the New Testament missionaries whose call the Holy Spirit has recorded for us in the Acts of the Apostles went out on his own initiative or in response to his own subjective sense of calling alone. In most cases, the subjective sense of call, though it may have been present, is not mentioned and is not the aspect of the call to which the Holy Spirit chose to draw our attention. In every case either the church with which they were associated or a missionary familiar with the work had a very considerable part to play. In other words, the objective call is stressed more than the subjective sense of calling.

And now for the evidence: Barnabas went to Antioch because his church sent him there (Acts 11. 22). Saul went to Antioch because Barnabas fetched him there (Acts 11. 25). Both men went out from Antioch, as a result of a joint decision made together with the other Antioch church leaders under the illumination of the Holy Spirit at a time of prayer and fasting (Acts 13. 2). Silas joined Paul at his invitation (Acts 15. 40) and so also did young Timothy (Acts 16. 3).

How do we apply this?

(*i*) What we find is not wild individualism or sensational forms of guidance, but God's people working, praying and planning together responsibly for the evangelization of the world. There is not just a selfish concern for any one individual's calling, but a dovetailing together of God's plan for many lives.

(*ii*) There does not seem to have been any stress on a general call for missionary volunteers in the New Testament. Missionaries went because their churches sent them, or because older missionaries fetched them.

(*iii*) It is an intensely personal matter between us and our Master that we should be willing to go anywhere for Him. But in deciding that this 'anywhere' should become a definite 'somewhere', both our home churches and the older missionaries have some say. Please note I am not trying to say that there was no subjective conviction on the part of the individual that the course of action suggested was the will of the Lord, but I am trying to point out that this is not the initial or the main element in the call as stressed in the New Testament, as some mistakenly think today and thus sit around waiting for a feeling, a vision or a verse. One suspects that Christians in those days found guidance no easier than we do today, judging by Acts 16. 6-10.

If this emphasis on the churches and the missionaries is found in The Acts, should we not make the same emphasis?

(a) *What does your church think?*

We are assuming that the church you belong to is sympathetic with missionary aims and that the leaders know you well enough because of your service and fellowship with them to discuss the matter with you. If the idea is met with enthusiasm—"We believe that you are suited and that God has been preparing you for this work, and we will back you up"—that surely will confirm your sense of being in the will of God. 'Hallelujah!' you shout. 'They think so too.' But if they say, "We should like to see a little more evidence of your usefulness here before we commit ourselves. . . ." Or even if they should say, "My dear chap, you are totally unsuitable!" Then you will have to take note of what they say. If they should say, "No, you are really far too valuable and we could not possibly spare you," that probably means you are just the sort of person who ought to go, but you will need to wait a while before they let you go! Look at the things which were said about Barnabas, Silas and even young

Timothy in Acts 11. 24; 15. 22, 32; 16. 2. If therefore you are an assistant minister, a Sunday School superintendent, or the leader of the young people's work, you are the very kind of person best qualified to go. Some churches may be apathetic about evangelizing in their own district, let alone to the uttermost part of the earth, and they will need much prayer if they are to back you up. Some may even be totally unsympathetic: if you are to stay at home, God may use you to transform the situation, but if you are going abroad, you may well wonder how much real support you will receive from your church.

(b) What do missionaries think?

Some of us are more than a little cautious about making too direct an approach to a missionary or a missionary society. We are almost afraid they will have us all signed on, weighed in, packed up and sent off before we can turn around. In forming an idea of 'where', there are many avenues to investigate without committing ourselves at all: missionary magazines to read, books about Christian work in other lands (look for realism, not glamour!), missionaries on furlough to listen to. In these ways we may begin to discover that certain types of work, geographical areas, or even societies have a special appeal to us. As we pray for guidance, perhaps one thing particularly will stand out. But even approaching missionary societies does not commit us—or them! Oddly enough, missionaries or their societies often seem to have a very healthy scepticism about our guidance. Not everybody who fancies himself climbing the Himalayas or who feels attracted by the glamour of tribal work is necessarily suitable for such work, and the high percentage of people who *feel* called to the glamorous fields makes one a little suspicious. Societies are not eager to saddle

themselves with impractical romantics who want to join and see the world at their expense. If you are wary about approaching them, you will find missions equally wary about you, and sizing you up very carefully. If they don't, that should make you more wary still!!! It's a bit like getting engaged to be married: both parties want to find out a good deal about the other before committing themselves. You will find out that no missionary society is perfect: and they will soon discover that not everything about you is found in your application papers!

A missionary society must train you and support you out of their meagre funds, whether you are a winner or a dud, and others will judge them by you! So no mission is knowingly going to take on a dud, no matter how spiritual it may be! Most of them have had enough experience of taking on people who were hard to live with or hard to live down. They are not going to be in a hurry to take us on, believe me, however highly we may value ourselves! On the other hand, some people have such an inferiority complex that they never give anybody a chance to say no. Once selected, missionaries turn out to be quite normal, and far from perfect people—as they were all along, really.

On the other hand, if the missionary society says: "Yes, we want you. There is a need in that place about which you have expressed an interest, for a person with just your qualifications. We know of no one else at the moment to fit that need. You seem to be the Lord's answer to our prayers," is not this dovetailing of the guidance of informed Christians with our own seeking after the Lord's will a very important part of guidance? If the Lord gives us a confirmatory verse as well, then this *cumulative guidance*, in fellowship with fellow-Christians, assures us of His will.

WHERE DOES GOD WANT ME?

Do you believe that the Lord has a plan for your life, that there are "good works prepared beforehand for us to walk in them" (Eph. 2. 10)? Why, yes, of course. Do you think He cares so little that He will not overrule any wrong decision on our part, especially when we are concerned to obey His will perfectly? If we are utterly willing to do His will, then He will guide us. I cannot do better than quote David Bentley-Taylor's words, "There is a common denominator, and that is the continual sense that a certain course of action is God's will for me and that I must do that and not anything else. It is this 'continual sense' which is really God's call, and it will remain with you long after little details of time, place and sign and verse have been forgotten in the distance of the years." Now you need just that same sense of call to go anywhere, whether to work in London or in the industrial north-east. Quoting Bentley-Taylor again, "The distinction between a call to South America and a call to Bermondsey is geographical, not spiritual." In other words, I can be certain that in various ways (and there is no stereotyped pattern for guidance) the Lord will make His way plain so that I fall in with His plan for my life. This is a very humbling and often overwhelming thing, but very wonderful because I have confidence that as His servant, I may count on His perfect direction and His unfailing support in all that I do for Him.

What if I approach a mission and they turn me down? Does that matter? What we are all trying to find out together is where each one of us is supposed to be, and where each one of us may serve Him best and please Him most. I may get turned down, but as with other proposals, I may ask again! The reason may be that I am not eligible, or that they are not interested in my particular gifts. They may have no need of student workers for Vietnam or Hong Kong, or perhaps no need of Bible translators or medical workers in Japan. This does not mean that I have not been guided, for here is some clear guidance for me. There is nothing unbiblical about being led by the 'Yes' or 'No' of my brethren, indeed it is what the New Testament encourages us to do. But a 'No' about one place is often the quickest route to a 'Yes' for another. As we have seen, the call to serve overseas is not different in kind from a call to serve in England —it differs only in destination. The Master is the same, His provision is the same, the motives are the same, the difficulties are often not so different, and the certainty of triumph in His Name is also the same. May God guide you as an individual and us as brethren together as we seek to find His will for each and every one of our lives, and all for the greatest glory of His great and glorious Name.

Check list for prayer

Am I willing to go anywhere?

Am I needed somewhere?

Am I eligible for service there?

How am I going to go, and for what
type of work?

Are others willing to send me there?

Is it His will, therefore, that I go?